for Harvey Phillips

Sonata No 1

for Tuba and Piano

(1959)

Alec Wilder

ISBN 978-0-634-02410-8

TRO ESSEX
MUSIC GROUP

for Harvey Phillips

Sonata For Tuba And Piano

I

ALEC WILDER

II

for Harvey Phillips

Sonata For Tuba And Piano

I

Tuba

Moderato ♩=c. 92

ALEC WILDER

II

for Harvey Phillips

Sonata For Tuba And Piano

I

Tuba

ALEC WILDER

II

III

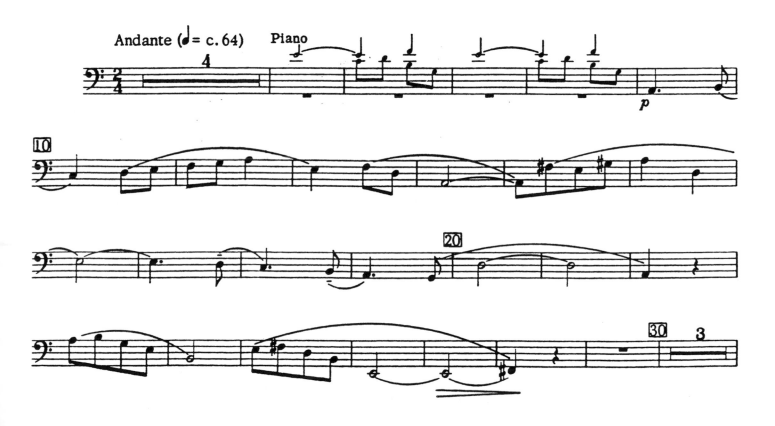

Tuba

Tuba

IV

III

IV